The INSIDE GUIDE

STEM IN SPORTS

STEM in Soccer

By Beatrice Harris

Cavendish Square

Published in 2025 by Cavendish Square Publishing, LLC
2544 Clinton Street Buffalo, NY 14224

Website: cavendishsq.com

Disclaimer: Portions of this work were originally authored by Emily Mahoney and published as *The Science of Soccer* (Sports Science). All new material this edition authored by Beatrice Harris.

All websites were available and accurate when this book was sent to press.

Library of Congress Cataloging-in-Publication Data

Names: Harris, Beatrice, author.
Title: STEM in soccer / Beatrice Harris.
Description: New York : Cavendish Square Publishing, 2025. | Series: The inside guide. STEM in sports | Includes index.
Identifiers: LCCN 2023053022 (print) | LCCN 2023053023 (ebook) | ISBN 9781502671318 (library binding) | ISBN 9781502671301 (paperback) | ISBN 9781502671325 (ebook)
Subjects: LCSH: Soccer–Juvenile literature. | Science–Juvenile literature.
Classification: LCC GV943.25 .H369 2025 (print) | LCC GV943.25 (ebook) | DDC 796.334083–dc23/eng/20231130
LC record available at https://lccn.loc.gov/2023053022
LC ebook record available at https://lccn.loc.gov/2023053023

Editor: Therese Shea
Copyeditor: Danielle Haynes
Designer: Deanna Lepovich

The photographs in this book are used by permission and through the courtesy of: Cover, p. 6 Fotokostic/Shutterstock.com; p. 4 mooinblack/Shutterstock.com; pp. 7, 10, 27 PeopleImages.com - Yuri A/Shutterstock.com; p. 9 kivnl/Shutterstock.com; p. 12 (soccer ball) Africa Studio/Shutterstock.com; p. 12 (inset) Marco Tulio/Shutterstock.com; p. 12 (main) fifg/Shutterstock.com; p. 13 Nomad_Soul/Shutterstock.com; p. 14 FOTOKITA/Shutterstock.com; p. 16 Master1305/Shutterstock.com; p. 17 Fabrizio Andrea Bertani/Shutterstock.com; p. 18 (angles) Tatgynsy/Shutterstock.com; p. 18 (main) dotshock/Shutterstock.com; p. 19 Dziurek/Shutterstock.com; p. 21 Dmytro Nychytalyuk/Shutterstock.com; p. 22 Jakkrit Orrasri/Shutterstock.com; p. 24 Victor Velter/Shutterstock.com; p. 25 Le Do/Shutterstock.com; p. 26 Skyshark Media/Shutterstock.com; p. 28 (top) Gorodenkoff/Shutterstock.com; p. 28 (bottom) matimix/Shutterstock.com; p. 29 (top) Oleksandr Osipov/Shutterstock.com; p. 29 (bottom) ph.FAB/Shutterstock.com.

Some of the images in this book illustrate individuals who are models. The depictions do not imply actual situations or events.

CPSIA compliance information: Batch #CSCSQ25: For further information contact Cavendish Square Publishing LLC at 1-877-980-4450.

Printed in the United States of America

CONTENTS

In many countries around the world, soccer is called football.

Chapter One

A STEM SPORT

Millions of soccer fans call this sport "the beautiful game." It's one of the most popular sports in the world and one which many people grow up playing.

How do players know how to kick the ball to hit the back of the net? How does the equipment the players wear affect their game? How can players get and stay in shape to play this fast-paced sport? We can answer these questions and more using STEM knowledge. STEM stands for science, **technology**, engineering, and math.

Physics and Forces

Physics is the branch of science that focuses on matter and energy and how they interact. Physicists—physics scientists—study forces and motion, and you can see examples of both in a soccer game. A force is a push or pull **exerted** on an object. You can see motion as soccer players and the ball move all over the field, changing position. However, not all motion in a soccer game is the same. Physics terms can help describe it.

Fast Fact

Another name for an object's change in position is displacement.

A soccer kick provides the force needed to put the ball into motion.

Fast Fact

Former striker Thierry Henry was possibly the fastest soccer player of all time. His top speed was nearly 24.4 miles (39.2 kilometers) per hour. That's a speed measurement.

Speed measures the rate at which something moves. Another way of saying this is the distance it moves in an amount of time. The direction an object moves doesn't matter. For example, a soccer player has speed when they run, even if they end up back where they started on the field.

Velocity measures the rate at which something changes its position. The direction of movement matters. To have velocity, an object needs to move away from where it started. A soccer player has velocity when

> **Fast Fact**
>
> A player whose velocity decreases over time can also be said to be accelerating, but this is negative acceleration.

they run down the field to score a goal. However, if they run back and forth and end up in the same position, their velocity is zero.

Acceleration is another way to measure motion. It's the measurement of how much an object's velocity changes over time. It's a vector quantity, which means direction is a part of it. When velocity increases over time, the object is said to be accelerating. A soccer player on offense accelerates when they increase their velocity to move faster. This is called positive acceleration.

Velocity is a vector quantity, which means it has a value (or number) and a direction. Speed is a scalar quantity, which means it has a value but doesn't require a direction.

Energy in Motion

When soccer players are moving down the field, they're using kinetic energy. Kinetic energy is the energy of motion. Every moving object has kinetic energy. When the object stops, it has potential energy. Potential energy is stored energy.

Types of Energy

Potential Energy

chemical energy—stored in atoms and molecules
example: batteries

mechanical energy—stored in objects by **tension**
example: springs

nuclear energy—stored in the nucleus of an atom
example: nuclear power

gravitational energy—stored in an object's height
example: roller coaster

Kinetic Energy

radiant energy—travels as **electromagnetic** waves
example: radio waves

thermal, or heat, energy—produced by movement of atoms and molecules
example: solar energy

motion energy—produced in the movement of objects
example: wind power

electrical energy—produced by atomic particles called electrons
example: lightning

sound energy—produced in waves by a vibrating object
example: musical instrument

Energy is all around us, converting to different forms.

TECHNOLOGY LIGHTS THE WAY

A British engineer named Laurence Kemball-Cook invented a technology based on the idea that one kind of energy can be transformed into another kind of energy. He came up with an energy-producing surface called Pavegen. When people walk or run on the surface, their kinetic energy is transformed into electrical energy, which can be stored in batteries and used to power lighting and other electrical devices. Pavegen on a soccer pitch, or field, is used to light the Morro da Mineira **stadium** in Brazil as well as other facilities, such as transportation centers.

Energy can't be created or destroyed, but it can change forms. This is the basis for the law of **conservation** of energy. The stops and starts of a soccer game provide plenty of examples of this physics law.

A soccer ball has kinetic energy when it's moving and potential energy when it's not.

Soccer players quickly learn how the ball acts on the field and in the air. Its shape has a lot to do with that.

ALL ABOUT THE BALL

Chapter Two

Soccer's connection to science is clear—but what about math? People use numbers to keep score, of course, and compare statistics, or number facts, such as minutes played, goals, and assists. However, there are other kinds of math too. Geometry is the branch of math that has to do with shapes, sizes, angles, and **dimensions**. Let's talk about the geometry of the soccer ball.

Spherical But Not a Sphere

The shape of many soccer balls is a truncated icosahedron, which is a shape with 60 vertices, or points. Soccer balls commonly have 12 pentagonal (5-sided) faces and 20 hexagonal (6-sided) faces. Each face is stitched or glued on as its own patch, or panel. These faces are curved, so the ball has a shape close to a sphere.

> **Fast Fact**
>
> A sphere is a three-dimensional object that is round in shape. It doesn't have edges or vertices, as soccer balls have.

Scientists have experimented with the number of panels a soccer ball is made with. These experiments have used wind tunnel tests and robotic kickers. The tests often compare the aerodynamics of different kinds of soccer balls.

A soccer ball is called a truncated icosahedron, which is an icosahedron with its tips truncated, or cut off.

Aerodynamics is a branch of science that studies the way air moves around objects and the way objects, such as soccer balls, move through the air.

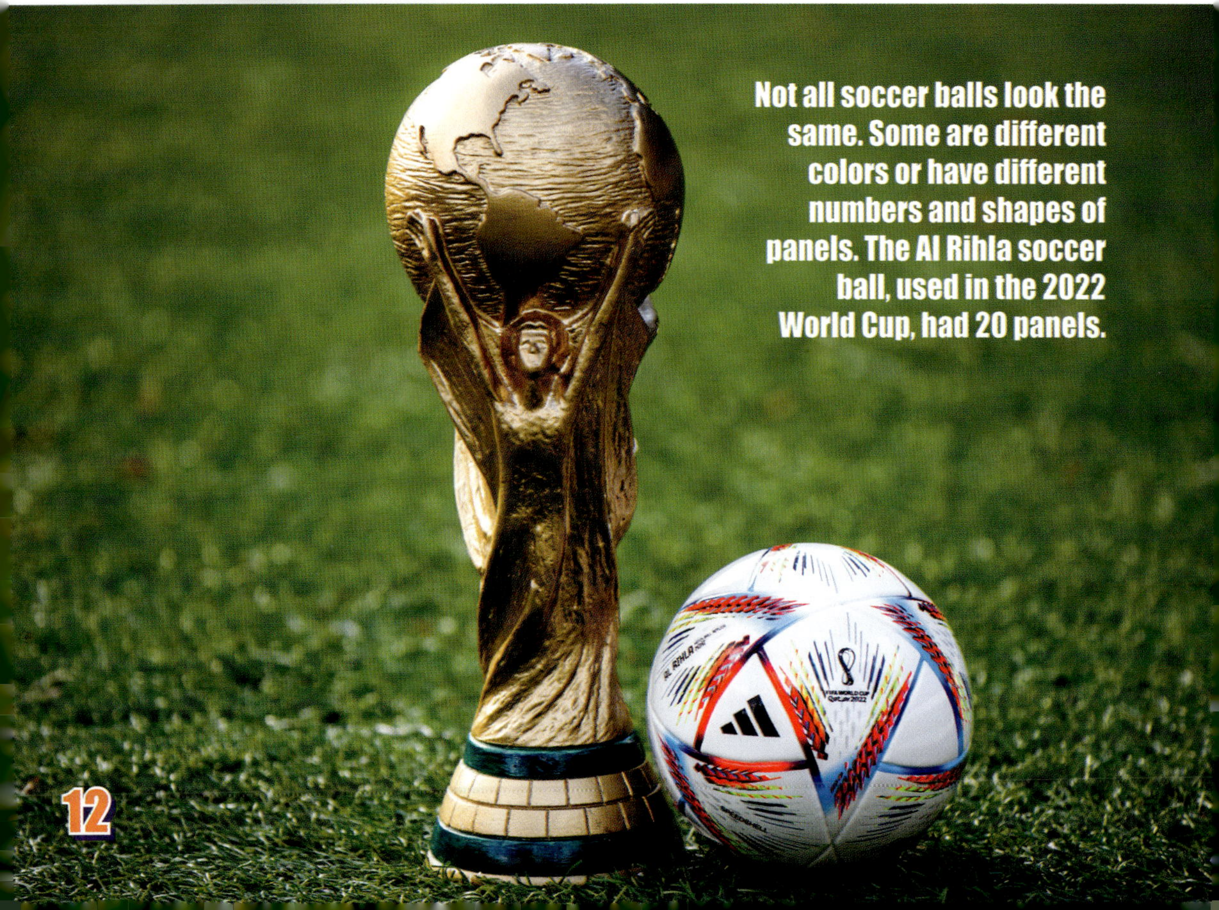

Not all soccer balls look the same. Some are different colors or have different numbers and shapes of panels. The Al Rihla soccer ball, used in the 2022 World Cup, had 20 panels.

The Air Inside

A soccer ball is more than the number of shapes on its surface. Air pressure also factors into the effectiveness of the ball. Even though air molecules are invisible, they have weight and take up space. The force of these air molecules pressing against an object or surface is air pressure.

FIFA rules say soccer balls should have an air pressure between about 8.5 pounds per square inch and 15.6 pounds per square inch, or 600 to 1,100 grams per square centimeter.

Fast Fact

FIFA stands for Fédération Internationale de Football Association. FIFA is an international governing body of soccer.

FRICTION IN THE GOAL

While no soccer goalkeeper, or goalie, has to wear gloves, nearly all high-level goalies do. Part of the reason is safety. A kicked soccer ball can travel faster than 70 miles (113 km) per hour. Catching or blocking a ball going that fast with bare hands really hurts! Goalie gloves also provide friction. Friction helps the goalie get a better grip on the ball, so it doesn't escape their hands and travel into the goal. Some goalies also think gloves that are just a bit moist—but not wet—provide even better grip.

Goalies don't run as much as players in other positions, but they need to be great jumpers.

Fast Fact

In 1855, Charles Goodyear made the first vulcanized rubber soccer balls.

Air pressure is created inside a container, or an object used to hold something, when air molecules get crammed together in one place. A soccer ball is a container because it holds air. A soccer ball has air molecules pumped into its center, which is a rubber **bladder**. The air pressure inside the ball increases as more air is pumped into the ball.

Outside Forces

The soccer ball moves when a force acts on it. A kick or a throw is called an applied force. A person kicking the ball is applying a force to put it in motion. Once the ball is in the air, it experiences other forces. Gravity is the force that pulls the ball (and all objects) down to Earth.

The ball also experiences friction in the air. Friction is a force of resistance when one object or substance slides or rolls over another. Friction in the air is called air resistance, or drag. The ball in the air feels resistance from air molecules all around it. They slow the ball. A ball rolling on the ground also experiences friction as it rolls over the surface of the field. It will eventually come to a stop.

If soccer players are taking a shot or making a long pass, they exert as much force as possible when they kick the ball.

Chapter Three

JUST FOR KICKS

Athletes can use science to figure out the best way to kick a soccer ball. A common saying in soccer is: "If you kick with your toe, who knows where it goes!" Soccer players kick the ball with the instep, or the flat part of the foot between the big toe and ankle. This gives the player more control over the direction of the ball than kicking with the toe because the instep has a greater surface area than the toe.

You can see the use of the instep in this photo.

Fast Fact

Anatomy is the study of body parts, such as muscles, joints, bones, and lungs. Physiology is the study of how these body parts work.

MORE MATH

An angle is made up of two lines that meet at a point. Angles are measured in degrees, which are represented by the symbol °. The most effective angle to get the most distance in a kick is about 45°. The foot that's not kicking the ball is just as important as the kicking foot. If a player wants the ball to go higher, they place their non-kicking foot slightly behind the ball. This creates a larger angle for the kick. If the foot is in front of or next to the ball, the angle will be smaller.

A player must practice kicking the ball at different angles to get it to their teammates or in the goal.

Fast Fact

If a soccer player can get their foot under the ball as they kick, the ball will go higher in the air.

When kicking a soccer ball, a player starts by approaching the ball from the side. This allows the hip to rotate, or turn, which creates more foot speed and force to move the ball. Hips can rotate because they're joints, which are body parts where bones come together.

From the Corner

A team is awarded a corner kick if the opposing team knocks the ball out of bounds on the goal line they're defending.

Corner kicks can be confusing for goalies because the ball's trajectory can change as it's moving.

Fast Fact

People who analyze, or study, soccer may use a kind of math called probability. They figure out the probability someone will score on a corner kick by dividing the number of times someone scores on a corner kick by their total number of attempts.

These kicks can be tricky because they're taken from the corner of the field, and many players are in the area where the ball usually lands.

There are two types of corner kicks: inswinging and outswinging. An inswinging kick curves outward from the goal line and then comes back in. It's useful because the trajectory, or path, of the ball places it closer to the net. An outswinging kick curves the ball in toward the goal line and then away from the goal. It's more difficult for the goalie to save, but also moves the ball farther from the net.

The Magnus Effect

Former soccer player David Beckham was famous for his skill at "bending" a soccer ball's trajectory around players to score. This skill actually has a scientific name: the Magnus effect.

The Magnus effect is caused by changes in velocity as an object moves through a liquid or gas, such as air. In soccer, the Magnus effect can be seen when a spinning soccer ball moves through the air.

The resistance, or drag, caused by the air around the ball slows the movement of the air on one side of the ball and speeds up the air's movement on the opposite side. This causes a difference in

The way a soccer ball's path curves when the Magnus effect is at work is commonly called a "banana kick" because the trajectory is curved like a banana.

air pressure, and the ball bends its trajectory toward the lower air pressure on the side where the air is moving faster.

The Magnus effect is used by athletes in other sports too. A baseball pitcher's curveball and a golfer's bending shot are two examples of this physics force at work.

Soccer players use knowledge of the human body to know how to exercise and what to eat to get the best performance out of their body. They can use it to stay safe too.

Chapter Four

SOCCER SAFETY

Except for the goalie, soccer players aren't allowed to use their hands to control the ball. However, using their head is acceptable. It's called heading the ball. It allows players to direct the ball while it's still in the air. However, it can also be dangerous.

Generally, it's recommended that players hit the ball with their forehead, not the top of their head. The player should also be moving toward the ball with their chin tucked toward their chest. All of this lessens the likelihood of headache or brain injury because the forehead is a thicker part of the skull.

Fast Fact

A U.S. high school sports study in the 2021-2022 school year showed that concussions happen more in girls' soccer than boys' soccer.

Avoiding Concussions

Neuroscientists, scientists who study the brain, say players should be careful after heading the ball. If they feel dizzy, have a headache or blurry vision, or feel sick to their stomach, they should be checked out by a trainer or coach immediately. These are signs of a concussion, which is a serious head injury. A concussion happens when

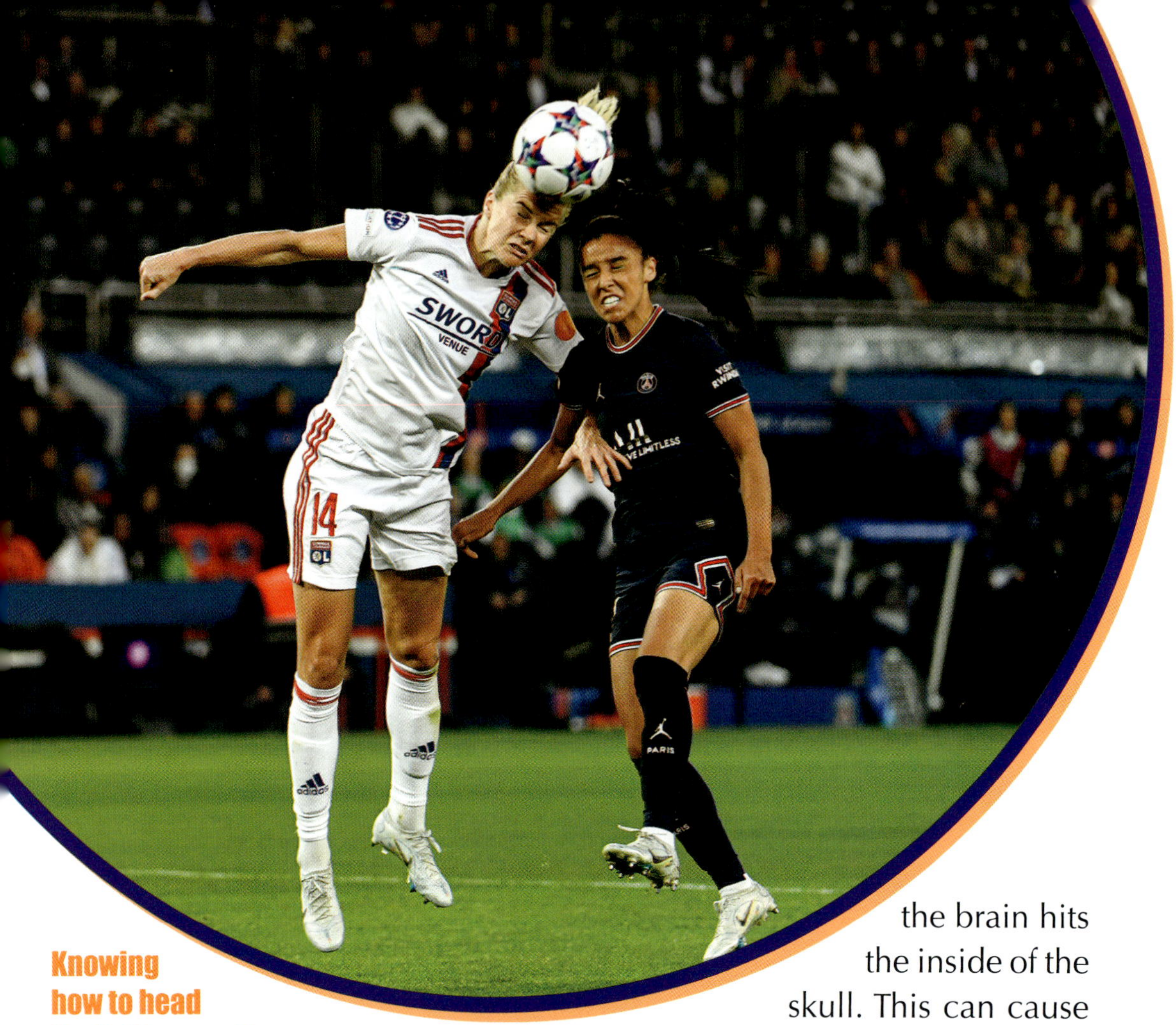

Knowing how to head the ball correctly can save players from serious head injuries. It can also help them score a goal.

the brain hits the inside of the skull. This can cause bruising or damage to blood vessels and nerves. The degree of the damage depends on the impact. Symptoms include headaches, balance problems, and behavior changes. Concussions can heal after several weeks.

To reduce the number of concussions in younger players, the organization U.S. Soccer no longer allows players 10 or younger to head the ball in practices or games. Players 11 and 12 years of age are required to limit their heading. Concussions can also happen when a player's head hits the ground or another player.

Gear That Guards

Players are allowed to wear headgear such as headbands to help prevent concussions. While the gear is made to distribute, or spread out, the force of an impact, many doctors and scientists don't think it offers enough protection to make a difference.

Another piece of gear does offer proven protection to the lower legs, however, which is why all FIFA players must wear them. Shin guards of some kind have been around since 1874. Technology has

Fast Fact

Shin guards come in different sizes. The top of it should start about 1 inch (2.5 centimeters) down from the knee. The bottom should end an inch or a bit more above the ankle.

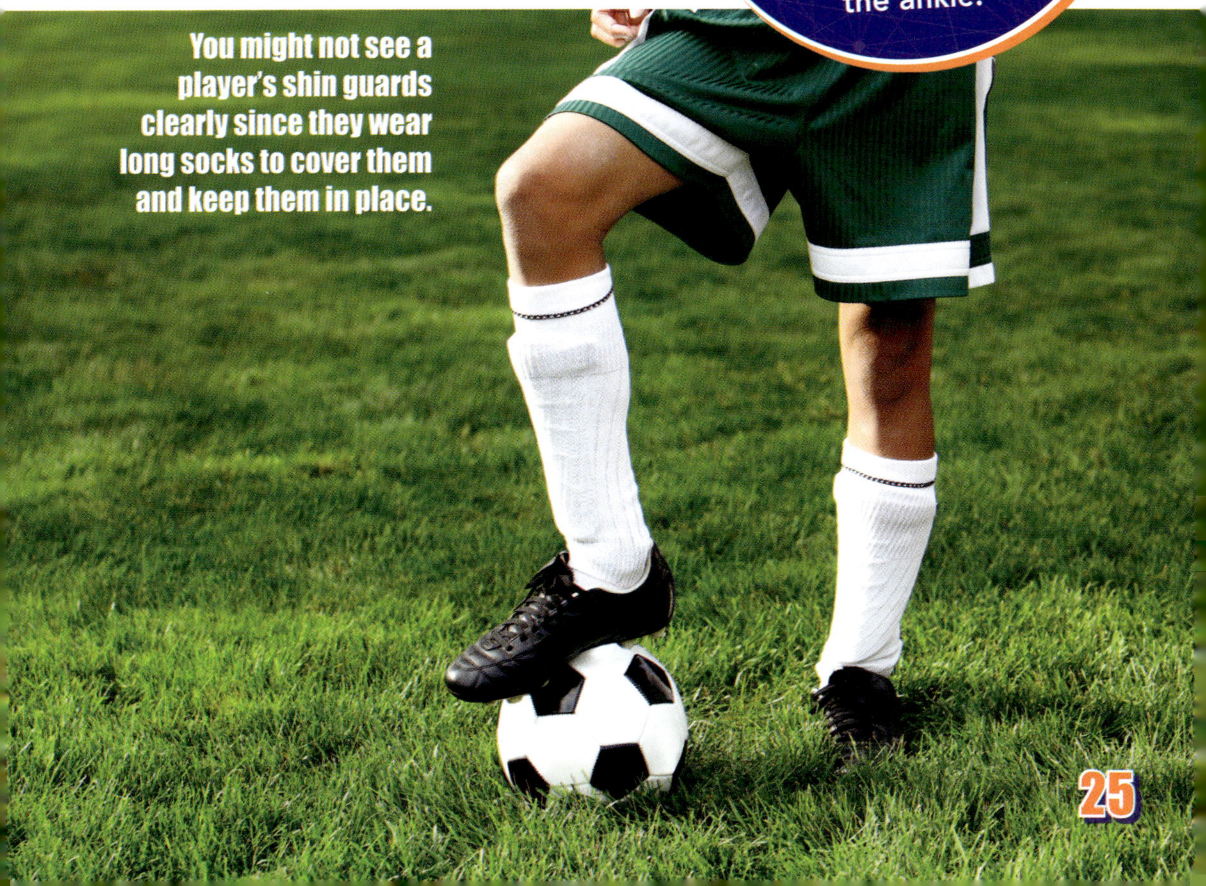

You might not see a player's shin guards clearly since they wear long socks to cover them and keep them in place.

ENGINEERING THE STADIUM

The best soccer teams in the world play in huge stadiums. Engineers use math, science, and technology to build soccer stadiums. One of the most impressive is England's Wembley Stadium. It has a partially **retractable** roof that allows for sunlight and **ventilation** inside. An arch 436 feet (133 meters) tall and 1,033 feet (315 m) long supports much of the weight of the roof. It's so tall it can be seen all across the city of London. Because of the arch, no pillars were needed to hold up the roof, allowing every fan to see the action without a pillar in their way.

Wembley Stadium seats 90,000 people.

Fast Fact

Wembley Stadium's field is made of a combination of natural grass and artificial turf, the name for human-made material that looks like grass.

provided newer materials such as carbon fiber, plastic, and foam, to make the guards more effective and comfortable.

Score with STEM

Soccer is even more exciting when you know the STEM behind it. The game is influenced not only by players' abilities but by invisible—though powerful—forces and visible technologies.

Smart soccer players know how to use their brain to help their team win. Fans can use STEM knowledge to get even more enjoyment from watching this beautiful game.

Soccer players can seem to ignore gravity with their athletic skills, but science is always at work on the field!

THINK ABOUT IT!

1. Choose three types of energy from the chart in Chapter 1 and give an example that can be found at a soccer game.

2. Explain how friction can help and hurt a player's performance in a game.

3. Can you think of a STEM idea that could help with injuries during a game?

4. Why do you think Wembley Stadium chose to use a mix of human-made and natural grass?

GLOSSARY

bladder: A soft bag filled with water or air.

conservation: The act of keeping a constant amount of something during a process of change.

dimension: Length, height, width, or depth.

electromagnetic: Having to do with a magnetic field that is produced by an electrical current.

exert: To put forth.

retractable: Able to pull back.

stadium: A large building where people gather to watch sporting events.

technology: Using science, engineering, and other industries to invent useful tools or to solve problems. Also, a machine, piece of equipment, or method created by technology.

tension: The amount something is stretched.

ventilation: Movement of air in and through a space.

vulcanize: To go through a process that uses heat and chemicals to make something harder and stronger.

FIND OUT MORE

Books

Buckley, James. *Soccer Atlas: A Journey Across the World and Onto the Soccer Field*. Mission Viejo, CA: QEB Publishing, 2021.

Kelley, K. C. *Soccer: Score with STEM!* Minneapolis, MN: Bearport Publishing Company, 2022.

Marquardt, Meg. *STEM in the World Cup*. Minneapolis, MN: Abdo Publishing, 2020.

Websites

Aerodynamics of Soccer
www.grc.nasa.gov/www/k-12/airplane/soccer.html
The U.S. space agency NASA offers information about the physics concepts behind soccer.

Angles in Soccer
thinkport.org/microsites/middleschoolmath/mmpt_int_angles-soccer.html
This site helps you understand the angles on the field.

Soccer: How to Play Basics
www.ducksters.com/sports/soccergameplay.php
Find out about the rules and positions of this beautiful game.

Publisher's note to educators and parents: Our editors have carefully reviewed these websites to ensure that they are suitable for students. Many websites change frequently, however, and we cannot guarantee that a site's future contents will continue to meet our high standards of quality and educational value. Be advised that students should be closely supervised whenever they access the internet.

INDEX